The Emotional Intelligence Secret

–

The Ugly Truth

M A. GRANT

ISBN-10: 1519791194
ISBN-13: 978-1519791191

British Library Catalogue in Publication Data:
A catalogue record for this book is available from the British Library.

www.icon-talent.org

DEDICATION

This book is dedicated to Tina, Olivia and Eva

CONTENTS

ACKNOWLEDGMENTS

From an early age I discovered the fascinating world of acknowledgments, since here was a way of getting closer to the writer and the artist. As I became an avid reader, my interest in acknowledgements grew, especially when I realized how difficult it is write a book of your own. There is something extremely difficult, even impossible, about naming everyone who has contributed to your work and to your personal development when you have been influenced by so many people, without at time even noticing their contribution or knowing they would have such a substantial impact.

I want to start by apologizing to anyone I may have omitted, I did not do so willingly or knowingly. There are some in particular who have given me license over the years to operate freely within their businesses in a way that has directly enriched this text.

My thanks and gratitude go out to you all.

Introduction

In an era defined by rapid technological advancements, globalization, and shifting societal norms, the complexities of human interaction have become more pronounced than ever. Navigating these complexities requires more than just cognitive intelligence; it demands a nuanced understanding of emotions—both our own and those of others. This is where emotional intelligence (EI) comes into play, offering a vital framework for enhancing personal and professional interactions.

Understanding Emotional Intelligence

Emotional intelligence is the capacity to recognize, comprehend, manage, and effectively utilize emotions in ourselves and in our interactions with others. Unlike traditional measures of intelligence, which focus on cognitive abilities, EI emphasizes emotional and social competencies that are crucial for effective communication, conflict resolution, and relationship building.

The concept of emotional intelligence was first introduced by psychologists Peter Salovey and John D. Mayer in the early 1990s, who defined it as a subset of social intelligence. However, it was Daniel Goleman's 1995 book, "Emotional Intelligence: Why It Can Matter More Than IQ," that brought the concept into mainstream awareness. Goleman's work highlighted the profound impact of EI on personal and professional success, sparking widespread interest and research into the field.

The Growing Importance of Emotional Intelligence

In today's interconnected world, emotional intelligence is more important than ever. Organizations are increasingly recognizing the value of EI in fostering a positive workplace culture, enhancing employee engagement, and driving business success. Leaders with high emotional intelligence are better equipped to inspire and motivate their teams, navigate complex interpersonal dynamics, and make decisions that reflect empathy and understanding.

For coaches, emotional intelligence is an essential tool for building rapport with clients, understanding their emotional landscapes, and guiding them toward meaningful personal and professional growth. In teams, EI promotes collaboration, innovation, and trust, creating an environment where diverse perspectives are not only accepted but celebrated.

On a personal level, emotional intelligence contributes to healthier relationships, improved mental health, and a greater sense of well-being. It empowers individuals to manage stress, communicate effectively, and navigate life's challenges with resilience and grace.

The Structure of This Book

This book is structured to provide a comprehensive exploration of emotional intelligence and its applications across various domains. We begin with a historical overview of EI, tracing its evolution from a theoretical concept to a practical tool for personal and professional development.

Subsequent chapters delve into the application of emotional intelligence in leadership, coaching, teams, and personal life. Each chapter provides insights, strategies, and practical examples to illustrate how EI can be harnessed to achieve success and fulfilment.

We will also introduce the GROW model as a tool for developing emotional intelligence skills. This model, which stands for Goals, Reality, Options, and Will, provides a structured approach for raising awareness, generating responsibility, and facilitating performance.

Real-World Examples and Case Studies

Throughout the book, we will present real-world examples and case studies that demonstrate the transformative power of emotional intelligence. These stories will illustrate how individuals and organizations have leveraged EI to overcome challenges, achieve their goals, and create positive change.

A Personal Journey

As you read this book, I encourage you to embark on a personal journey of self-discovery and growth. Reflect on your own experiences with emotional intelligence and consider how you can apply the principles and strategies discussed in these pages to enhance your life and the lives of those around you.

Emotional intelligence is not just a skill to be learned; it is a way of being that can profoundly impact every aspect of your life. By cultivating EI, you can unlock your full potential, build stronger relationships, and contribute to a more empathetic and connected world.

A Call to Action

The journey to mastering emotional intelligence is ongoing, and the rewards are immeasurable. Whether you are a leader seeking to inspire your team, a coach guiding others toward their goals, or an individual striving for personal growth, emotional intelligence offers a pathway to greater fulfilment and success.

As part of the "Ugly Truth Series," this book aims to uncover the often-overlooked realities of emotional intelligence—its challenges, its transformative power, and its essential role in our lives. As we explore the depths of emotional intelligence together, I invite you to embrace the opportunities for growth and transformation that lie ahead. Let us embark on this journey with curiosity, openness, and a commitment to becoming the best versions of ourselves.

Chapter 1 – The History of EQ

Understanding the history of emotional intelligence (EI) offers crucial insights into how this concept has evolved and why it is pivotal in personal and professional realms today. From its early theoretical foundations to its present-day applications, the journey of EI illustrates its profound impact on our understanding of human behaviour and interaction.

Early Foundations

The exploration of intelligence beyond cognitive abilities began in the early 20th century. Psychologist Edward Thorndike was one of the first to introduce the idea of "social intelligence" in 1920, which he described as the ability to understand and manage people and to act wisely in human relations. This early work laid the groundwork for future research into the emotional and social dimensions of intelligence, suggesting that understanding and navigating social environments were as crucial as intellectual capabilities.

The Emergence of Emotional Intelligence

The term "emotional intelligence" was formally introduced by psychologists Peter Salovey and John D. Mayer in a 1990 paper titled "Emotional Intelligence," published in the journal Imagination, Cognition, and Personality. They defined emotional intelligence as "a form of social intelligence that involves the ability to monitor one's own and others' feelings and emotions, to discriminate among them, and to use this information to guide one's thinking and actions."

Salovey and Mayer's model of emotional intelligence included four key components:

1. Perceiving Emotions: The ability to accurately recognize emotions in oneself and others, which is the foundational skill upon which other EI skills are built.

2. Using Emotions to Facilitate Thought: The capacity to harness emotions to prioritize thinking and problem-solving, allowing emotions to guide cognitive processes.

3. Understanding Emotions: The ability to

comprehend emotional language and the signals conveyed by emotions, including recognizing how emotions evolve over time.

4. Managing Emotions: The skill to regulate emotions in oneself and others, promoting emotional and intellectual growth.

Their groundbreaking work provided a structured framework for understanding how emotions influence cognitive processes and behaviour, paving the way for further exploration and application of EI.

Popularization by Daniel Goleman

The concept of emotional intelligence gained widespread recognition and popular appeal with the publication of Daniel Goleman's 1995 book, "Emotional Intelligence: Why It Can Matter More Than IQ." Goleman expanded on Salovey and Mayer's work, emphasizing the role of EI in workplace success, leadership, and personal relationships. He posited that emotional intelligence could be more significant than traditional IQ in determining success in life.

Goleman's model of emotional intelligence included five components:

1. Self-awareness: Recognizing and understanding one's own emotions and their impact on others.

2. Self-regulation: The ability to control or redirect disruptive emotions and impulses and adapt to changing circumstances.

3. Motivation: A passion for work that goes beyond money and status, driven by inner ambition.

4. Empathy: The ability to understand the emotional makeup of other people and treat them according to their emotional reactions.

5. Social Skills: Proficiency in managing relationships and building networks.

His book became a bestseller, sparking global interest in the study and application of emotional intelligence across various fields, including business, education, and psychology. Goleman's work highlighted the practical implications of EI, making it accessible to a broader audience and encouraging individuals and organizations to incorporate EI into their development strategies.

Advancements in Research and Application

Since Goleman's influential work, research on emotional intelligence has flourished, leading to the development of various models and assessment tools. The Mayer-Salovey-Caruso Emotional Intelligence Test (MSCEIT) and the Emotional Quotient Inventory (EQ-i) are among the most widely used measures of EI today. These tools have provided empirical support for the concept and have been instrumental in validating the significance of EI in various contexts.

In the business world, emotional intelligence has become a key focus of leadership development programs, with companies recognizing its importance in enhancing employee engagement, teamwork, and organizational culture. Leaders with high EI are seen as more effective in managing change, fostering innovation, and creating inclusive work environments.

In education, emotional intelligence is being integrated into curricula to help students develop the social and emotional skills needed for success in school and beyond. Programs aimed at increasing students' EI have been shown to improve academic performance, reduce behavioural problems, and enhance social interactions.

Criticisms and Challenges

Despite its popularity, the concept of emotional intelligence has faced criticism and challenges. Some researchers argue that EI lacks a clear and consistent definition, leading to difficulties in measurement and assessment. Others question the validity of EI as a distinct form of intelligence, suggesting that it may overlap with personality traits or other psychological constructs.

Critics also point out that the commercial success of EI-related books and programs may have outpaced the scientific evidence supporting the concept. However, the continued interest and research in emotional intelligence underscore its relevance and potential. As our understanding of the human mind and emotions evolves, so too does our appreciation for the role of EI in shaping our lives and interactions.

Conclusion

The history of emotional intelligence is a journey of discovery and innovation, reflecting our growing awareness of the complex interplay between emotions and cognition. From its early conceptualization as social intelligence to its current status as a critical component of personal and professional development, EI has transformed the way we understand and engage with the world around us.

As we move forward in this book, we will explore how emotional intelligence can be applied to enhance leadership, coaching, teamwork, and personal growth. By understanding the history and evolution of EI, we can better appreciate its significance and harness its power to create positive change in our lives and the lives of others.

Chapter 2 – Understanding EQ

Emotional intelligence (EI) represents a transformative approach to understanding human behaviour, emphasizing the role of emotions in our interactions and decision-making processes. This chapter provides an in-depth exploration of the components of emotional intelligence, its significance across various domains, and how it contrasts with traditional intelligence.

Defining Emotional Intelligence

Emotional intelligence is the capacity to be aware of, control, and express one's emotions, and to handle interpersonal relationships judiciously and empathetically. It is a crucial factor influencing personal and professional success, as it involves the ability to navigate social complexities and make informed decisions. EI is not just about being in touch with your emotions; it's about using this awareness to manage behaviour and relationships effectively.

The Components of Emotional Intelligence

Emotional intelligence is typically broken down into several key components, each of which plays a vital role in how we interact with the world:

1. **Self-Awareness**:

    - **Description**: Self-awareness is the ability to recognize and understand your own emotions and how they affect your thoughts and behaviour. It involves an honest assessment of one's strengths and weaknesses and a clear sense of one's values and goals.

    - **Importance**: Self-awareness is the foundation of emotional intelligence, as it allows individuals to understand their emotional triggers and manage their responses effectively. It leads to better decision-making, enhances personal growth, and fosters authenticity in interactions.

    - **Development Strategies**: To enhance self-awareness, individuals can practice mindfulness, seek feedback from others, and engage in reflective practices such as journaling.

2. **Self-Regulation**:

- **Description**: Self-regulation is the ability to control or redirect disruptive emotions and impulses and to think before acting. It involves staying calm under pressure, maintaining composure, and being adaptable to change.

- **Importance**: Individuals with strong self-regulation skills can manage their emotions in healthy ways, take initiative, and follow through on commitments. It fosters trust and integrity in relationships and professional settings.

- **Development Strategies**: Techniques such as deep breathing, meditation, and cognitive restructuring can help individuals improve their self-regulation skills.

3. **Motivation**:

- **Description**: Motivation in the context of emotional intelligence refers to the intrinsic drive to achieve goals for personal fulfilment rather than external rewards. It involves a passion for work that goes beyond money and status.

- **Importance**: Emotionally intelligent individuals are often highly motivated, optimistic, and committed to achieving their objectives. They are resilient in the face of setbacks and maintain a positive outlook, which inspires others.

- **Development Strategies**: Setting meaningful goals, maintaining a positive attitude, and focusing on intrinsic rewards can enhance motivation.

4. **Empathy**:

- **Description**: Empathy is the ability to understand and share the feelings of others. It involves being aware of others' emotions, needs, and concerns, and responding appropriately.

- **Importance**: Empathy is crucial for building strong relationships, managing conflicts, and fostering a supportive environment. It allows individuals to connect with others on a deeper level and enhances communication.

- **Development Strategies**: Active listening, perspective-taking, and practicing compassion can help individuals develop empathy.

5. **Social Skills**:

- **Description**: Social skills are the tools used to interact effectively with others. They include communication, conflict resolution, and relationship-building skills.

- **Importance**: Individuals with strong social skills can work well in teams, communicate clearly, and manage relationships effectively. These skills are essential for leadership, collaboration, and networking.

- **Development Strategies**: Improving communication techniques, learning conflict resolution strategies, and engaging in social activities can enhance social skills.

The Significance of Emotional Intelligence

Emotional intelligence is significant for several reasons:

- **Enhanced Communication**: EI improves communication by allowing individuals to express themselves clearly and understand others' perspectives. This leads to more effective interactions and reduces misunderstandings, fostering a positive and collaborative environment.

- **Better Relationships**: Individuals with high EI

are better equipped to build and maintain healthy relationships. They can empathize with others, manage conflicts constructively, and create a positive social environment. This leads to stronger personal and professional connections.

- **Improved Decision-Making**: Emotional intelligence allows individuals to make balanced decisions by considering both emotional and rational factors. It helps in assessing situations objectively and choosing the best course of action, leading to better outcomes in personal and professional settings.

- **Increased Resilience**: EI enhances resilience by enabling individuals to manage stress and adapt to change. Emotionally intelligent individuals are better able to cope with challenges and bounce back from adversity, maintaining their well-being and productivity.

- **Leadership and Influence**: Leaders with high emotional intelligence can inspire and motivate others, manage stress and conflict, and create a positive organizational culture. EI is a key differentiator for effective leadership.

Emotional Intelligence vs. Traditional Intelligence

Emotional intelligence differs from traditional intelligence (IQ) in several ways:

- **Focus**: While IQ focuses on cognitive abilities such as logical reasoning, problem-solving, and analytical skills, EI emphasizes emotional and social competencies. Both are important, but they serve different purposes in achieving success and fulfilment.

- **Measurement**: IQ is typically measured through standardized tests that assess cognitive abilities, whereas EI is assessed through self-report questionnaires, behavioural observations, and performance-based tests that evaluate emotional and social skills.

- **Application**: IQ is often associated with academic and professional success, while EI is linked to personal and interpersonal success. Emotional intelligence is increasingly recognized as a critical factor in achieving overall success and well-being, as it influences how we interact with others and navigate life's challenges.

Conclusion

Understanding emotional intelligence is essential for navigating the complexities of modern life. By developing the components of EI—self-awareness, self-regulation, motivation, empathy, and social skills—individuals can enhance their communication, relationships, decision-making, and resilience. As we continue to explore the applications of emotional intelligence in leadership, coaching, teams, and personal life, it becomes clear that EI is a powerful tool for achieving success and fulfilment in all areas of life.

Chapter 3 – EQ in Leadership

In the realm of leadership, emotional intelligence (EI) is not just an asset; it is a necessity. As organizations and teams become more complex, the ability to navigate interpersonal dynamics, inspire others, and manage change is paramount. This chapter explores how emotional intelligence enhances leadership effectiveness, its connection to values-based leadership, and its alignment with Daniel Goleman's concept of Primal Leadership.

The Role of Emotional Intelligence in Leadership

Emotional intelligence in leadership involves the ability to understand and manage one's own emotions, as well as the emotions of others. Leaders with high EI can create a positive organizational culture, foster collaboration, and drive performance. Here are key ways EI impacts leadership:

1. **Building Trust and Relationships**:

   - **Importance**: Trust is the foundation of effective leadership. Leaders who demonstrate empathy, transparency, and authenticity can build strong, trusting relationships with their teams.

   - **Application**: By actively listening to team members and acknowledging their feelings, leaders can create an environment where employees feel valued and understood. This involves open-door policies, regular check-ins, and creating spaces for open dialogue.

2. **Effective Communication**:

   - **Importance**: Communication is a core leadership skill. Emotionally intelligent leaders can convey their vision clearly and inspire others to follow.

   - **Application**: Leaders should practice open and honest communication, adapting their style to meet the needs of different audiences. This includes being attuned to non-verbal cues, such as body language and tone of voice, and providing constructive feedback that encourages growth and development.

3. **Conflict Resolution**:

    *   **Importance**: Conflicts are inevitable in any organization. EI equips leaders with the skills to manage and resolve conflicts effectively, minimizing disruptions and maintaining team harmony.

    *   **Application**: Leaders can use empathy to understand different perspectives and facilitate discussions that lead to mutually beneficial solutions. This involves remaining neutral, focusing on the issue rather than personal attacks, and encouraging collaborative problem-solving.

4. **Decision-Making**:

    *   **Importance**: Emotional intelligence enhances decision-making by allowing leaders to balance logic and emotion. This leads to more informed and empathetic choices.

    *   **Application**: Leaders should consider the emotional impact of their decisions on stakeholders and strive to align decisions with organizational values and goals. This involves seeking diverse perspectives, weighing the pros and cons, and being transparent about the decision-making

process.

5. **Adaptability and Change Management**:

- **Importance**: In today's fast-paced world, adaptability is crucial. Leaders with high EI can navigate change with resilience and guide their teams through transitions.

- **Application**: By maintaining a positive outlook and demonstrating flexibility, leaders can inspire confidence and motivate their teams to embrace change. This involves clear communication of the change process, addressing concerns empathetically, and providing support throughout the transition.

Emotional Intelligence and Values-Based Leadership

Values-based leadership is an approach that emphasizes leading with integrity, authenticity, and a commitment to ethical principles. Emotional intelligence is integral to this style of leadership, as it involves aligning actions with core values and fostering a culture of trust and respect.

1. **Alignment with Core Values**:

- **Description**: Emotionally intelligent leaders are aware of their values and ensure that their actions reflect these principles. This alignment builds credibility and trust within the organization.

- **Application**: Leaders can articulate their values and integrate them into decision-making processes. By doing so, they set a standard for ethical behaviour and inspire others to follow suit.

2. **Fostering a Values-Driven Culture**:

- **Description**: Leaders with high EI create environments where values are openly discussed and integrated into daily operations. This fosters a sense of purpose and belonging among team members.

- **Application**: Leaders can encourage open dialogue about values and recognize individuals who exemplify these principles in their work. This reinforces the importance of values and strengthens organizational culture.

Primal Leadership and Emotional Intelligence

Daniel Goleman's concept of Primal Leadership emphasizes the emotional dimension of leadership and the impact of leaders' emotional states on their teams. According to Goleman, emotionally intelligent leaders can create resonance, a positive emotional climate that enhances performance and well-being.

1. **Creating Resonance**:

    - **Description**: Resonant leaders use emotional intelligence to connect with their teams on an emotional level, fostering a sense of harmony and shared purpose.

    - **Application**: Leaders can create resonance by being attuned to the emotional needs of their team members and responding with empathy and encouragement. This involves recognizing achievements, providing support during challenges, and maintaining a positive attitude.

2. **Leadership Styles in Primal Leadership**:

    - **Description**: Goleman identifies six leadership styles—visionary, coaching, affiliative, democratic, pacesetting, and commanding—that are influenced by emotional intelligence.

    - **Application**: Leaders can adapt their style based on the needs of their team and the situation. For example, a visionary style may be effective in setting a new direction, while a coaching style can help develop individual potential.

Case Studies and Examples

1. **Case Study: Transformational Leadership**:

    - **Scenario**: A CEO of a tech company faced the challenge of leading a major organizational change due to a merger. Employees were anxious about job security and adapting to new processes.

    - **Application of EI**: The CEO used emotional intelligence to lead the transition by holding town hall meetings to communicate the vision and address concerns. By actively listening to employee feedback and involving them in the change process, the CEO fostered trust and collaboration. This approach resulted in a smoother transition and increased employee engagement.

2. **Example: Conflict Resolution**:

    - **Scenario**: A manager in a marketing firm observed ongoing tension between two team members, which was affecting team performance.

    - **Application of EI**: The manager applied empathy and active listening to mediate the conflict. By meeting with each team member individually to understand their perspectives and then facilitating a joint discussion, the manager encouraged open communication and mutual understanding. The resolution strengthened team cohesion and improved overall productivity.

3. **Example: Decision-Making**:

- **Scenario**: A project leader had to decide whether to allocate additional resources to a struggling project or cut losses and redirect efforts elsewhere.

- **Application of EI**: The leader considered both the logical aspects and the emotional impact on the team. By consulting with team members and stakeholders, the leader gathered diverse perspectives and assessed the potential outcomes. The decision to provide additional support was communicated transparently, with a focus on learning and growth, which motivated the team to successfully turn the project around.

Conclusion

Emotional intelligence is a cornerstone of effective leadership, deeply intertwined with values-based leadership and Primal Leadership concepts. By cultivating EI, leaders can enhance their ability to communicate, build relationships, resolve conflicts, and navigate change. As we continue to explore the applications of emotional intelligence in coaching, teams, and personal life, it becomes clear that EI is an essential tool for achieving success and fulfilment in leadership roles.

M A. Grant

Chapter 4 – Emotional Intelligence in Coaching

Coaching is a powerful tool for personal and professional development, and emotional intelligence (EI) plays a crucial role in enhancing the effectiveness of coaching relationships. By integrating EI into coaching practices, coaches can foster deeper connections with clients, facilitate meaningful change, and empower individuals to reach their full potential. This chapter explores how emotional intelligence can be applied in coaching, including its impact on key coaching skills and processes.

The Role of Emotional Intelligence in Coaching

Emotional intelligence in coaching involves the ability to understand and manage one's own emotions, as well as the emotions of clients. Coaches with high EI can create a supportive and empathetic environment that encourages clients to explore their thoughts and feelings openly. Here are key ways EI impacts coaching:

1. **Building Rapport and Trust**:

    - **Importance**: Establishing a strong rapport is essential for effective coaching. Coaches who demonstrate empathy, authenticity, and genuine interest in their clients' well-being can build trust and create a safe space for exploration.

    - **Application**: Coaches can build rapport by actively listening, showing empathy, and being fully present during coaching sessions. This involves acknowledging clients' emotions and validating their experiences. Trust is further strengthened through consistency, reliability, and maintaining confidentiality.

2. **Effective Questioning**:

    - **Importance**: Asking powerful questions is a core coaching skill that helps clients gain insights and identify solutions. Emotionally intelligent coaches can frame questions that resonate with clients' emotions and encourage self-reflection.

- **Application**: Coaches can use open-ended questions that invite clients to explore their feelings and motivations. Questions like "How does this situation make you feel?" or "What values are influencing your decision?" can deepen clients' understanding of their emotions. Effective questioning also involves probing deeper into clients' responses to uncover underlying beliefs and assumptions.

3. **Active Listening**:

   - **Importance**: Active listening is crucial for understanding clients' perspectives and fostering a sense of connection. Coaches with high EI can listen beyond words, picking up on emotional cues and underlying concerns.

   - **Application**: Coaches should practice active listening by maintaining eye contact, nodding, and providing verbal affirmations. Reflecting back what clients say and summarizing key points can demonstrate understanding and encourage further exploration. Active listening also involves being attuned to non-verbal signals, such as body language and tone of voice, which can provide additional insights into clients' emotions.

4. **Empathic Responding**:

- **Importance**: Empathic responding involves acknowledging and validating clients' emotions, which can foster trust and openness. Emotionally intelligent coaches can respond empathetically to clients' feelings and experiences.

- **Application**: Coaches can use empathic responses such as "I can see how that situation could be challenging" or "It sounds like you're feeling overwhelmed." These responses show understanding and support clients in processing their emotions. Empathic responding also involves offering reassurance and encouragement, helping clients feel supported throughout their coaching journey.

5. **Facilitating Change and Growth**:

- **Importance**: Coaching aims to facilitate change and growth, and EI is instrumental in helping clients navigate their emotions and take action. Coaches with high EI can guide clients in setting goals and developing strategies for personal and professional growth.

- **Application**: Coaches can use the GROW model (Goals, Reality, Options, Will) to structure coaching sessions and support clients in achieving their objectives. Emotional intelligence enhances each stage of the model by incorporating empathy and emotional awareness into goal-setting and problem-solving.

The GROW Model and Emotional Intelligence

The GROW model is a widely used coaching framework that helps clients set and achieve goals. Emotional intelligence enhances the effectiveness of the GROW model by integrating emotional awareness and empathy into each stage:

1. **Goals**:

    - **Description**: The first stage involves helping clients define clear and meaningful goals. Emotionally intelligent coaches can guide clients in identifying goals that align with their values and aspirations.

    - **Application**: Coaches can ask questions like "What would achieving this goal mean to you emotionally?" to help clients connect with their motivations and aspirations. By exploring the emotional significance of goals, coaches can help clients establish a strong sense of purpose and commitment.

2. **Reality**:

- **Description**: In this stage, coaches help clients assess their current situation and identify any obstacles. EI enables coaches to explore clients' emotions and perceptions, providing a holistic understanding of their reality.

- **Application**: Coaches can use empathic listening to understand clients' feelings about their current situation and encourage honest self-assessment. By acknowledging emotions such as fear or frustration, coaches can help clients gain clarity and develop a realistic view of their circumstances.

3. **Options**:

- **Description**: Coaches work with clients to explore possible strategies and solutions. Emotional intelligence allows coaches to facilitate creative thinking and encourage clients to consider the emotional impact of different options.

- **Application**: Coaches can ask questions like "How do you feel about each option?" to help clients evaluate the emotional implications of their choices. By exploring the pros and cons of various options, coaches can support clients in developing a balanced and informed decision-making process.

4. **Will**:

- **Description**: The final stage involves supporting clients in committing to action and creating a plan. EI helps coaches motivate clients and address any emotional barriers to taking action.

- **Application**: Coaches can use motivational techniques and empathic encouragement to help clients build confidence and take decisive steps toward their goals. By addressing potential fears or doubts, coaches can empower clients to overcome obstacles and maintain momentum.

In-Depth Case Studies and Examples

1. **Case Study: Career Transition Coaching**:

- **Scenario**: A client named Sarah was seeking a career change from finance to a more creative field. Despite her desire for change, she struggled with self-doubt and fear of failure.

- **Application of EI**: The coach began by building rapport and trust, creating a safe space for Sarah to express her fears and

M A. Grant

aspirations. Through effective questioning, the coach helped Sarah explore her motivations and the emotional significance of pursuing a creative career. By actively listening and responding empathetically, the coach validated Sarah's feelings and provided reassurance. During the GROW model process, the coach guided Sarah in setting realistic goals, assessing her current skills and resources, and exploring creative options that aligned with her values. The coach addressed Sarah's self-doubt by helping her reframe negative thoughts and build confidence through small, achievable steps. With the coach's support, Sarah developed a clear action plan and successfully transitioned into a fulfilling creative role.

2. **Example: Leadership Development Coaching**:

- **Scenario**: A senior manager named James wanted to improve his leadership skills and build stronger relationships with his team. He faced challenges in communication and conflict resolution.

- **Application of EI**: The coach applied the GROW model, using emotional intelligence to guide James in setting leadership goals that aligned with his values. Through active listening and empathic responding, the coach helped James develop emotional awareness and identify areas for improvement. By exploring James's communication style and conflict resolution strategies, the coach facilitated discussions on the emotional impact of his actions on team dynamics. The coach provided feedback and role-playing exercises to enhance James's social skills and empathy. As a result, James became more effective in managing conflicts, fostering collaboration, and inspiring his team.

3. **Example: Personal Growth Coaching**:

- **Scenario**: A client named Lisa aimed to improve her work-life balance and reduce stress. She felt overwhelmed by competing demands and struggled to prioritize self-care.

- **Application of EI**: The coach used emotional intelligence to help Lisa identify stressors and explore her emotional responses. By facilitating discussions about values and priorities, the coach empowered Lisa to set boundaries and implement self-care practices. Through the GROW model, the coach supported Lisa in setting realistic goals for work-life balance, assessing her current commitments, and exploring options for delegating tasks and scheduling downtime. The coach provided empathic encouragement and accountability, helping Lisa maintain her self-care routine and achieve a healthier balance.

Conclusion

Emotional intelligence is a powerful asset in coaching, enhancing the coach's ability to connect with clients, facilitate meaningful change, and empower individuals to achieve their goals. By integrating EI into coaching practices, coaches can create supportive and empathetic environments that foster growth and transformation. As we continue to explore the applications of emotional intelligence in teams and personal life, it becomes clear that EI is an essential tool for achieving success and fulfilment in coaching relationships.

Chapter 5 – EQ in Teams

In today's collaborative work environments, the success of a team often hinges not just on the individual competencies of its members, but on their collective ability to work together effectively. Emotional intelligence (EI) plays a pivotal role in enhancing team dynamics, fostering a culture of collaboration, and driving collective success. This chapter explores how emotional intelligence can be applied within teams, highlighting its impact on communication, conflict resolution, and overall team performance.

The Importance of Emotional Intelligence in Teams

Emotional intelligence within teams involves the collective ability to recognize, understand, and manage emotions, both individually and as a group. Teams with high EI are better equipped to navigate interpersonal dynamics, adapt to change, and achieve their goals. Here are key ways EI impacts team effectiveness:

1. **Enhanced Communication**:

    - **Importance**: Effective communication is the cornerstone of successful teamwork. Teams with high EI can communicate openly and honestly, reducing misunderstandings and fostering a positive work environment.

    - **Application**: Team members can practice active listening, express themselves clearly, and be attuned to non-verbal cues. Encouraging open dialogue and feedback allows teams to address issues proactively and maintain alignment. Regular team meetings and open forums can provide platforms for sharing ideas and addressing concerns.

2. **Conflict Resolution**:

    - **Importance**: Conflicts are inevitable in any team setting. EI equips teams with the skills to manage and resolve conflicts constructively, minimizing disruptions and maintaining cohesion.

    - **Application**: Teams can use empathy to understand different perspectives and facilitate discussions that lead to mutually beneficial solutions. Establishing ground rules for respectful communication and conflict resolution can help teams navigate disagreements effectively. Conflict resolution training and mediation sessions can further support teams in managing conflicts.

3. **Building Trust and Collaboration**:

- **Importance**: Trust is essential for effective collaboration. Teams with high EI can build strong, trusting relationships, enabling them to work together more efficiently and creatively.

- **Application**: Teams can build trust by being reliable, transparent, and supportive. Encouraging collaboration through team-building activities and shared goals fosters a sense of unity and purpose. Celebrating team achievements and recognizing individual contributions can strengthen trust and collaboration.

4. **Adaptability and Resilience**:

- **Importance**: In today's fast-paced work environments, adaptability is crucial. Teams with high EI can navigate change with resilience and maintain productivity during transitions.

- **Application**: Teams can develop adaptability by embracing change, learning from setbacks, and maintaining a positive outlook. Encouraging a growth mindset and continuous learning helps teams stay agile and innovative. Regular debriefs and reflection sessions can help teams learn from experiences and improve future performance.

5. **Diversity and Inclusion**:

  - **Importance**: Diverse teams bring a wealth of perspectives and ideas. EI enables teams to appreciate and leverage diversity, creating an inclusive environment where all voices are heard.

  - **Application**: Teams can promote inclusion by valuing different perspectives, encouraging participation, and addressing biases. Celebrating diversity and fostering a culture of respect enhances team creativity and problem-solving. Diversity training and inclusive leadership practices can further support teams in creating an inclusive environment.

Strategies for Developing Emotional Intelligence in Teams

To harness the power of emotional intelligence, teams must be committed to collective growth and development.

Here are strategies for enhancing EI within teams:

1. **Team Workshops and Training**:

    - **Practice**: Teams can participate in workshops and training sessions focused on developing emotional intelligence skills, such as communication, empathy, and conflict resolution. These sessions can be tailored to address specific team needs and challenges.

2. **Regular Check-Ins and Feedback**:

    - **Practice**: Establishing regular check-ins and feedback sessions allows teams to address issues, celebrate successes, and continuously improve their dynamics. Feedback should be constructive and focused on behaviours and outcomes rather than personal attributes.

3. **Emotional Climate Assessments**:

    - **Practice**: Conducting assessments of the team's emotional climate can help identify areas for improvement and track progress over time. These assessments can include surveys, interviews, and observation to gather insights into team dynamics.

4. **Role-Playing and Simulations**:

    - **Practice**: Engaging in role-playing exercises and simulations can help teams practice EI skills in a safe environment and prepare for real-world scenarios. These activities can enhance empathy, communication, and problem-solving skills.

5. **Mindfulness and Stress Management**:

   - **Practice**: Incorporating mindfulness practices and stress management techniques can enhance team members' self-awareness and emotional regulation. Mindfulness sessions, meditation, and stress-relief activities can help teams manage stress and maintain focus.

In-Depth Case Studies and Examples

1. **Case Study: Cross-Functional Team Collaboration**:

   - **Scenario**: A cross-functional team in a tech company was tasked with developing a new product. The team faced challenges due to differing priorities and communication styles among members from engineering, marketing, and sales.

   - **Application of EI**: The team participated in EI workshops to improve communication and empathy. By practicing active listening and open dialogue, team members learned to appreciate each other's perspectives and align their goals. Regular feedback sessions helped the team address conflicts promptly and maintain cohesion. As a result, the team successfully launched the product, leveraging their diverse expertise and collaborative spirit. The team also implemented a rotating leadership model, allowing members from different functions to lead meetings and decision-making processes, further enhancing cross-functional understanding and collaboration.

2. **Example: Remote Team Effectiveness**:

    - **Scenario**: A remote team in a global organization struggled with maintaining connection and trust due to geographical and cultural differences.

    - **Application of EI**: The team implemented virtual team-building activities and regular video check-ins to strengthen relationships. By fostering an inclusive culture and encouraging participation, the team enhanced communication and collaboration. The use of digital tools for real-time feedback and recognition helped the team stay engaged and motivated, leading to improved performance and job satisfaction. The team also established a buddy system, pairing members from different locations to facilitate cultural exchange and support.

3. **Example: Conflict Resolution in Project Teams**:

   - **Scenario**: A project team in a construction company experienced tension due to tight deadlines and resource constraints.

   - **Application of EI**: The team established ground rules for respectful communication and conflict resolution. By using empathy and problem-solving techniques, the team addressed disagreements constructively and developed solutions that met project goals. The team's ability to navigate conflicts effectively contributed to the successful completion of the project on time and within budget. The team also conducted post-project reviews to reflect on their conflict resolution strategies and identify areas for improvement.

Conclusion

Emotional intelligence is a critical component of effective teamwork, enhancing communication, collaboration, and resilience. By developing EI within teams, organizations can foster a culture of trust, inclusivity, and innovation. As we continue to explore the applications of emotional intelligence in personal life, it becomes clear that EI is an essential tool for achieving success and fulfilment in team settings.

Chapter 6 – EQ in Personal Life

Emotional intelligence (EI) is not just a professional asset; it's a vital skill that can transform personal life, enhancing relationships, improving mental well-being, and fostering personal growth. By understanding and applying EI in everyday situations, individuals can navigate life's challenges with greater ease and fulfilment. This chapter explores how emotional intelligence can be applied in personal life, highlighting its impact on relationships, self-awareness, and overall well-being.

The Role of Emotional Intelligence in Personal Life

Emotional intelligence in personal life involves the ability to recognize, understand, and manage one's own emotions, as well as the emotions of others. It enables individuals to connect more deeply with themselves and those around them, leading to more meaningful and satisfying relationships. Here are key ways EI impacts personal life:

1. **Enhancing Relationships**:

    - **Importance**: Healthy relationships are built on understanding, trust, and effective communication. EI helps individuals navigate interpersonal dynamics and build stronger connections.

    - **Application**: By practicing active listening and empathy, individuals can better understand the emotions and perspectives of others. This fosters open communication and mutual respect, strengthening relationships with family, friends, and partners. Regularly expressing appreciation and gratitude can further enhance relationship bonds.

2. **Improving Self-Awareness**:

    - **Importance**: Self-awareness is the foundation of personal growth and self-improvement. EI helps individuals gain insight into their emotions, behaviours, and motivations.

    - **Application**: Regular self-reflection and

mindfulness practices can enhance self-awareness. By recognizing emotional triggers and patterns, individuals can make more conscious choices and align their actions with their values. Keeping a journal to document thoughts and emotions can provide valuable insights into personal growth.

3. **Managing Stress and Emotions**:

- **Importance**: Life's challenges often bring stress and emotional upheaval. EI equips individuals with the skills to manage stress and regulate emotions effectively.

- **Application**: Techniques such as deep breathing, meditation, and cognitive restructuring can help individuals manage stress and maintain emotional balance. By developing emotional resilience, individuals can navigate adversity with greater ease. Establishing a regular routine that includes relaxation and self-care activities can support emotional well-being.

4. **Fostering Empathy and Compassion**:

- **Importance**: Empathy and compassion are essential for building meaningful connections and contributing positively to the community. EI enhances individuals' ability to empathize with others and act with kindness.

- **Application**: Engaging in volunteer work, practicing gratitude, and participating in community activities can foster empathy and compassion. These practices promote a sense of belonging and purpose. Developing an understanding of different cultures and perspectives can further enhance empathy.

5. **Promoting Personal Growth and Fulfilment**:

- **Importance**: Personal growth is a lifelong journey of self-discovery and development. EI supports individuals in setting and achieving personal goals, leading to greater fulfilment.

- **Application**: By setting meaningful goals and reflecting on personal values, individuals can pursue growth and self-improvement. Continuous learning and embracing new experiences contribute to a fulfilling life. Seeking feedback from others and being open to change can further support personal growth.

Strategies for Developing Emotional Intelligence in Personal Life

To harness the power of emotional intelligence, individuals must be committed to personal growth and development.

Here are strategies for enhancing EI in personal life:

1. **Mindfulness and Meditation**:

   - **Practice**: Mindfulness practices and meditation can enhance self-awareness and emotional regulation. Regular mindfulness exercises help individuals stay present and attuned to their emotions. Techniques such as body scans, mindful breathing, and guided imagery can be incorporated into daily routines.

2. **Journaling and Self-Reflection**:

   - **Practice**: Keeping a journal and engaging in self-reflection can provide insights into emotions and behaviours. Writing about experiences and feelings helps individuals process emotions and gain clarity. Setting aside time for regular reflection can deepen self-understanding and support personal growth.

3. **Active Listening and Empathy Exercises**:

   - **Practice**: Practicing active listening and empathy exercises can improve interpersonal skills. Engaging in meaningful conversations and seeking to understand others' perspectives fosters connection. Role-playing exercises and empathy-building activities can further enhance these skills.

4. **Stress Management Techniques**:

- **Practice**: Incorporating stress management techniques, such as yoga, exercise, and relaxation exercises, can enhance emotional resilience. These practices help individuals cope with stress and maintain well-being. Creating a balanced lifestyle that includes physical activity, healthy nutrition, and adequate rest supports emotional health.

5. **Goal Setting and Personal Development**:

- **Practice**: Setting personal goals and pursuing continuous learning can promote personal growth. Individuals can explore new hobbies, take courses, and seek opportunities for self-improvement. Developing a personal development plan and tracking progress can provide motivation and direction.

In-Depth Case Studies and Examples

1. **Case Study: Strengthening Family Bonds**:

- **Scenario**: A parent named Alex wanted to improve communication and strengthen relationships with their teenage children, who were becoming increasingly distant.

- **Application of EI**: Alex began by setting

aside regular family time to engage in activities that everyone enjoyed. During these sessions, Alex practiced active listening, allowing the children to express their thoughts and feelings without interruption. By acknowledging their emotions and validating their experiences, Alex fostered trust and understanding. The family established a weekly family meeting to discuss any issues, share successes, and plan activities together. This approach led to stronger bonds, improved communication, and a more harmonious family environment.

2. **Example: Managing Stress and Anxiety**:

- **Scenario**: A college student named Jamie struggled with stress and anxiety during exam periods, impacting their academic performance and well-being.

- **Application of EI**: Jamie attended a stress management workshop and learned techniques such as mindfulness meditation and progressive muscle relaxation. By practicing these techniques daily, Jamie improved emotional regulation and reduced anxiety. Jamie also set realistic study goals, prioritized tasks, and incorporated regular breaks and self-care activities into their routine. By seeking support from friends and utilizing campus resources, Jamie developed a strong support network. These strategies led to better stress management, improved academic performance, and enhanced overall well-being.

3. **Example: Building Empathy and Community Engagement**:

- **Scenario**: An individual named Sam wanted to contribute positively to their community and build empathy through meaningful engagement.

- **Application of EI**: Sam volunteered at a local shelter, where they interacted with individuals from diverse backgrounds. By listening to their stories and understanding their challenges, Sam developed a deeper sense of empathy and compassion. Sam also joined a community group focused on cultural exchange, participating in discussions and activities that broadened their perspective. These experiences enhanced Sam's understanding of different cultures and fostered a sense of belonging and purpose. Sam's involvement in community activities also inspired others to engage in volunteer work, creating a ripple effect of positive impact.

Conclusion

Emotional intelligence is a transformative skill that can enhance personal life, improving relationships, self-awareness, and overall well-being. By developing EI, individuals can navigate life's challenges with greater ease and achieve personal growth and fulfilment. As we continue to explore the applications of emotional intelligence in various domains, it becomes clear that EI is an essential tool for living a meaningful and satisfying life.

Chapter 7 – Developing EQ Skills

Developing emotional intelligence (EI) is a lifelong journey that requires commitment, practice, and self-awareness. By enhancing EI skills, individuals can improve their relationships, decision-making, and overall well-being. This chapter provides a comprehensive guide to developing emotional intelligence, offering practical strategies and exercises to strengthen each component of EI.

Understanding the Components of Emotional Intelligence

Before diving into development strategies, it's essential to revisit the core components of emotional intelligence:

1. **Self-Awareness**: The ability to recognize and understand your own emotions and how they affect your thoughts and behaviour.

2. **Self-Regulation**: The ability to control or redirect disruptive emotions and impulses and to think before acting.

3. **Motivation**: A passion for work that goes beyond money and status, driven by inner ambition.

4. **Empathy**: The ability to understand and consider others' feelings, especially when making decisions.

5. **Social Skills**: Proficiency in managing relationships and building networks.

Strategies for Developing Emotional Intelligence

To develop emotional intelligence, individuals can engage in targeted practices and exercises that enhance each component:

Self-Awareness

1. **Mindfulness Meditation**:

   - **Practice**: Engage in daily mindfulness meditation to increase awareness of your thoughts and emotions. Focus on the present moment and observe your emotions without judgment.

   - **Exercise**: Set aside 10-15 minutes each day for mindfulness meditation. Sit comfortably, close your eyes, and focus on your breath. Notice any thoughts or emotions that arise, and gently bring your focus back to your breath.

2. **Journaling**:

- **Practice**: Keep a daily journal to document your emotions, thoughts, and experiences. Reflect on emotional triggers and patterns to gain insights into your behavior.

- **Exercise**: Write in your journal each evening, reflecting on the day's events and your emotional responses. Consider questions like "What emotions did I experience today?" and "What triggered these emotions?"

3. **Feedback Seeking**:

- **Practice**: Seek feedback from trusted friends, family, or colleagues to gain an external perspective on your emotional responses and behavior.

- **Exercise**: Identify specific areas where you'd like feedback, such as your communication style or emotional reactions. Ask for constructive feedback and use it to enhance your self-awareness.

Self-Regulation

1. **Breathing Techniques**:

- **Practice**: Use deep breathing exercises to calm your mind and body during stressful situations. Techniques such as diaphragmatic breathing can help regulate emotions.

- **Exercise**: Practice diaphragmatic breathing by inhaling deeply through your nose, allowing your abdomen to expand, and exhaling slowly through your mouth. Repeat for several minutes to achieve a state of calm.

2. **Cognitive Restructuring**:

- **Practice**: Challenge and reframe negative thoughts to change your emotional response. Identify cognitive distortions and replace them with more balanced perspectives.

- **Exercise**: When you notice negative thoughts, ask yourself questions like "Is this thought based on facts?" and "What is a more balanced way to view this situation?" Write down alternative thoughts that promote a positive mindset.

3. **Impulse Control Exercises**:

- **Practice**: Practice delaying gratification and controlling impulses by setting small goals and rewarding yourself for achieving them.

- **Exercise**: Choose a small goal, such as resisting the urge to check your phone during work hours. Set a reward for achieving the goal, such as a favorite snack or activity. Gradually increase the difficulty of your goals to strengthen impulse control.

Motivation

1. **Goal Setting**:

    - **Practice**: Set clear, achievable goals that align with your values and passions. Break down larger goals into smaller, manageable steps to maintain motivation.

    - **Exercise**: Use the SMART criteria (Specific, Measurable, Achievable, Relevant, Time-bound) to set goals. Write down your goals and create an action plan with specific steps and deadlines.

2. **Visualization**:

    - **Practice**: Visualize the successful achievement of your goals to enhance motivation and commitment. Imagine the positive emotions associated with reaching your objectives.

    - **Exercise**: Spend a few minutes each day visualizing yourself achieving your goals. Picture the steps you need to take and the emotions you'll feel when you succeed. Use this visualization to reinforce your motivation.

3. **Positive Affirmations**:

- **Practice**: Use positive affirmations to reinforce your self-belief and motivation. Repeat affirmations that align with your goals and aspirations.

- **Exercise**: Write down a list of positive affirmations, such as "I am capable of achieving my goals" or "I am resilient and adaptable." Repeat these affirmations daily, either silently or aloud, to boost your confidence and motivation.

Empathy

1. **Active Listening**:

- **Practice**: Practice active listening by giving your full attention to others, maintaining eye contact, and responding thoughtfully. Reflect back what you hear to ensure understanding.

- **Exercise**: During conversations, focus on listening more than speaking. Use phrases like "What I hear you saying is..." to confirm your understanding and show empathy.

2. **Perspective-Taking**:

- **Practice**: Put yourself in others' shoes to understand their feelings and viewpoints. Engage in exercises that challenge you to see situations from different perspectives.

- **Exercise**: Choose a recent interaction where you disagreed with someone. Write down the situation from their perspective, considering their emotions and motivations. Reflect on how this perspective-taking influences your understanding and empathy.

3. **Compassionate Communication**:

- **Practice**: Use compassionate communication techniques to express empathy and understanding. Focus on non-judgmental language and validate others' emotions.

- **Exercise**: Practice using "I" statements, such as "I feel concerned when..." to express your feelings without blaming others. Validate others' emotions by acknowledging their experiences and showing understanding.

Social Skills

1. **Networking**:

- **Practice**: Build and maintain a network of supportive relationships. Attend social events, join clubs or organizations, and engage in community activities.

- **Exercise**: Set a goal to connect with a new person each week, whether through a social event, online platform, or mutual connection. Focus on building genuine relationships by expressing interest in others and offering support.

2. **Conflict Resolution**:

- **Practice**: Develop conflict resolution skills by practicing negotiation and problem-solving techniques. Focus on finding win-win solutions and maintaining positive relationships.

- **Exercise**: When conflicts arise, use a structured approach to address the issue. Identify the root cause, explore potential solutions, and collaborate with others to reach a resolution. Practice active listening and empathy throughout the process.

3. **Team Collaboration**:

- **Practice**: Participate in team projects and collaborative activities to enhance your social skills. Embrace diverse perspectives and contribute to group success.

- **Exercise**: Volunteer for a team project or join a group activity. Practice effective communication, active listening, and collaboration to achieve shared goals. Reflect on the experience and identify areas for improvement.

Integrating Emotional Intelligence into Daily Life

To fully develop emotional intelligence, individuals must integrate EI practices into their daily routines:

1. **Daily Reflection**:

   - **Practice**: Set aside time each day for reflection on your emotional experiences and interactions. Consider what went well and what couldbe improved.

   - **Exercise**: Create a daily reflection ritual, such as journaling or meditation. Use this time to review your day, identify emotional patterns, and set intentions for improvement.

2. **Regular Practice**:

   - **Practice**: Consistently engage in EI exercises and practices to build habits and reinforce skills. Set reminders or create a schedule to ensure regular practice.

   - **Exercise**: Develop a weekly plan that

includes specific EI activities, such as mindfulness meditation, active listening, and goal setting. Track your progress and adjust your plan as needed.

3. **Continuous Learning**:

- **Practice**: Pursue opportunities for continuous learning and personal development. Read books, attend workshops, and seek mentorship to expand your understanding of EI.

- **Exercise**: Identify areas of EI you want to explore further and seek out resources, such as books, courses, or webinars. Engage in discussions with others to share insights and learn from different perspectives.

Conclusion

Developing emotional intelligence is a transformative journey that can enhance every aspect of your life. By committing to the practices and strategies outlined in this chapter, individuals can strengthen their EI skills and achieve greater success, fulfilment, and well-being. As we continue to explore the applications of emotional intelligence, it becomes clear that EI is an essential tool for personal and professional growth.

Chapter 8 – Case Studies

Understanding the theoretical aspects of emotional intelligence (EI) is essential, but seeing how these concepts play out in real-world scenarios provides invaluable insights. This chapter presents a series of detailed case studies that illustrate the transformative power of emotional intelligence across various contexts, including leadership, coaching, teams, and personal life.

Case Study 1: Transformative Leadership in a Tech Company

Scenario: InnovateTech, a mid-sized tech company, faced challenges with employee engagement and a lack of innovation. The company had experienced rapid growth, but this led to a top-down management style that stifled creativity and collaboration.

Application of EI:

- **Self-Awareness and Self-Regulation**: The CEO, Lisa, recognized through employee surveys and feedback sessions that her leadership style was perceived as controlling. She began a process of self-reflection and enlisted the help of an executive coach to develop greater self-awareness. Lisa worked on self-regulation by delegating more responsibilities and trusting her team to take ownership of their projects, reducing her tendency to micromanage.

- **Empathy and Social Skills**: Lisa implemented regular town hall meetings and one-on-one check-ins to actively listen to employee concerns and ideas. By showing empathy and understanding, she built stronger relationships and trust within the organization. She also encouraged managers to practice active listening and empathy in their interactions with team members.

- **Outcome**: Over time, InnovateTech saw a significant increase in employee engagement and innovation. Teams felt more empowered to propose new ideas, leading to successful product launches and improved market competitiveness. The company also noticed a decrease in turnover rates and an improvement in overall employee satisfaction.

Case Study 2: Coaching for Career Transition

Scenario: Emily, a corporate finance professional, sought coaching services to transition to a career in social entrepreneurship. Despite her passion for social causes, she struggled with self-doubt and uncertainty about making such a significant career change.

Application of EI in Coaching:

- **Empathy and Active Listening**: Emily's coach, Sarah, created a safe space for her to express her fears and aspirations. By practicing active listening and empathy, Sarah validated Emily's emotions and helped her gain clarity on her motivations. They explored Emily's underlying fears, such as the fear of financial instability and the pressure to meet societal expectations.

- **Goal Setting and Motivation**: Using the GROW model, Sarah guided Emily in setting clear goals for her career transition. They broke down the transition into manageable steps, such as networking with social entrepreneurs, attending relevant workshops, and exploring volunteer opportunities. By aligning her goals with her values, Emily found renewed motivation and confidence.

- **Outcome**: With Sarah's support, Emily successfully transitioned to a role in social entrepreneurship, founding a nonprofit focused on sustainable development. She gained confidence in her abilities and found fulfilment in aligning her career with her values. Emily's story inspired others in her network to pursue their passions, leading to a ripple effect of positive change.

Case Study 3: Enhancing Team Dynamics in a Marketing Firm

Scenario: Creative Solutions, a marketing firm, was struggling with internal conflicts and communication breakdowns, affecting their ability to meet project deadlines and deliver quality work. The team consisted of diverse individuals with varying communication styles and work preferences.

Application of EI:

- **Conflict Resolution and Empathy**: The team participated in EI workshops facilitated by an external consultant to enhance their conflict resolution skills. Through role-playing exercises and empathy-building activities, team members learned to understand each other's perspectives and work collaboratively. They practiced active listening and developed strategies for addressing conflicts constructively.

- **Building Trust and Collaboration**: The team implemented regular feedback sessions and team-building activities to strengthen relationships and foster trust. They established ground rules for communication, such as using "I" statements and focusing on solutions rather than blame.

- **Outcome**: The team's improved communication and collaboration led to more efficient project management and higher-quality deliverables. The positive team dynamics also contributed to increased job satisfaction and reduced turnover. As a result, Creative Solutions experienced a boost in client satisfaction and business growth.

Conclusion

These detailed case studies demonstrate the profound impact of emotional intelligence across various contexts. Whether in leadership, coaching, or team dynamics, EI provides the tools to enhance communication, foster collaboration, and drive personal and professional growth. As we continue to explore the applications of emotional intelligence, it becomes clear that developing EI is a transformative journey that can lead to lasting success and fulfilment.

Chapter 9 – The Secret

As we reach the conclusion of our exploration into emotional intelligence (EI), it is clear that EI is a transformative force with the potential to profoundly impact both personal and professional spheres. Throughout this book, we have delved into the history, components, and applications of emotional intelligence, illustrating its significance and providing practical strategies for development. This chapter synthesizes the key insights and lessons learned, offering a holistic view of how EI can lead to a more fulfilling and successful life, while revealing the "EQ Secret - the Ugly Truth."

The Transformative Power of Emotional Intelligence

Emotional intelligence is more than just a set of skills; it is a way of being that enhances our interactions with ourselves and others. By developing EI, individuals can:

1. **Enhance Relationships**: EI fosters empathy, active listening, and effective communication, which are essential for building and maintaining strong relationships. Whether in personal life or professional settings, emotionally intelligent individuals can navigate interpersonal dynamics with greater ease and understanding.

2. **Improve Self-Awareness and Self-Regulation**: Through self-reflection and mindfulness, individuals can gain a deeper understanding of their emotions and behaviours. This self-awareness is the foundation for self-regulation, allowing individuals to manage their emotional responses and make conscious choices aligned with their values.

3. **Drive Motivation and Personal Growth**: EI helps individuals connect with their intrinsic motivations and set meaningful goals. By aligning actions with values and passions, individuals can achieve personal growth and fulfilment. The ability to motivate oneself and others is a hallmark of emotionally intelligent leaders and influencers.

4. **Foster Collaboration and Team Success**: In team settings, EI enhances communication, conflict resolution, and collaboration. Teams with high EI can leverage diverse perspectives, build trust, and work together effectively to achieve

shared objectives. This leads to improved performance, innovation, and job satisfaction.

5. **Navigate Change and Challenges**: Emotional intelligence equips individuals with the resilience and adaptability needed to navigate life's challenges and changes. By managing stress and maintaining a positive outlook, emotionally intelligent individuals can overcome obstacles and thrive in dynamic environments.

The EQ Secret - The Ugly Truth

While emotional intelligence is often celebrated for its positive impact, the "EQ Secret - the Ugly Truth" reveals that developing EI is not without its challenges. Here are some of the less-discussed aspects of emotional intelligence:

1. **Emotional Vulnerability**: Cultivating emotional intelligence requires individuals to confront and embrace their vulnerabilities. This can be uncomfortable and challenging, as it involves facing difficult emotions and acknowledging personal limitations.

2. **Continuous Effort and Commitment**: Developing EI is a lifelong journey that demands ongoing effort and dedication. It is not a one-time achievement but a continuous process of growth and self-improvement.

3. **Balancing Empathy and Boundaries**: While empathy is a core component of EI, it is essential

to maintain healthy boundaries. Empathizing with others should not come at the expense of one's well-being. Striking a balance between empathy and self-care is crucial.

4. **Navigating Complex Interpersonal Dynamics**: High EI can lead to increased awareness of complex interpersonal dynamics, which can be both a blessing and a burden. Emotionally intelligent individuals may find themselves more attuned to conflicts and tensions, requiring them to navigate these situations with care.

5. **Resistance to Change**: Despite the benefits of EI, some individuals and organizations may resist change and growth. Emotionally intelligent individuals may encounter resistance from others who are not ready or willing to embrace EI principles.

Integrating Emotional Intelligence into Daily Life

To fully realize the benefits of emotional intelligence, individuals must integrate EI practices into their daily routines. This involves:

- **Continuous Learning and Development**: Emotional intelligence is a lifelong journey that requires ongoing commitment and practice. Engaging in regular self-reflection, seeking feedback, and pursuing opportunities for personal development are essential for enhancing EI skills.

- **Mindfulness and Presence**: Mindfulness practices help individuals stay present and attuned to their emotions. By cultivating mindfulness, individuals can improve self-awareness and emotional regulation, leading to more intentional and effective interactions.

- **Empathy and Compassion**: Building empathy and compassion involves actively listening to others, seeking to understand diverse perspectives, and responding with kindness. These practices strengthen relationships and contribute to a more empathetic and connected world.

- **Goal Setting and Motivation**: Setting clear, achievable goals and aligning them with personal values fosters motivation and fulfilment. Visualization and positive affirmations can reinforce commitment and drive progress toward desired outcomes.

The Future of Emotional Intelligence

As we look to the future, the importance of emotional intelligence (EI) will only continue to grow. In an increasingly interconnected and complex world, the ability to understand and manage emotions is crucial for success and well-being. The future of EI is poised to be shaped by several key trends and developments:

Integration with Technology and AI

The rapid advancement of technology and artificial intelligence (AI) presents both opportunities and challenges for emotional intelligence. As AI systems become more sophisticated, there is a growing interest in developing emotionally intelligent machines that can recognize and respond to human emotions. This integration could enhance human-computer interactions, making technology more intuitive and responsive to our emotional needs.

However, the rise of AI also underscores the importance of uniquely human qualities, such as empathy, creativity, and emotional insight. As routine tasks become automated, the demand for emotional intelligence in the workforce will increase. Individuals who can harness EI to build relationships, foster collaboration, and drive innovation will be highly valued.

Emotional Intelligence in Education

The future of emotional intelligence is closely linked to its integration into educational systems. As educators recognize the importance of EI in student development, there is a growing emphasis on incorporating social-emotional learning (SEL) programs into curricula. These programs aim to equip students with the skills to manage emotions, build relationships, and make responsible decisions.

By fostering emotional intelligence from a young age, educational institutions can prepare students for the complexities of the modern world. SEL programs not only enhance academic performance but also contribute to improved mental health and well-being. As these programs gain traction, they have the potential to transform the way we educate future generations.

Emotional Intelligence in the Workplace

In the workplace, emotional intelligence is increasingly recognized as a critical factor for leadership and organizational success. As businesses navigate the challenges of globalization, remote work, and diverse workforces, EI will be essential for fostering inclusive and collaborative cultures.

Organizations that prioritize emotional intelligence in their leadership development programs can create environments where employees feel valued, motivated, and engaged. Emotionally intelligent leaders are adept at managing change, resolving conflicts, and inspiring teams to achieve their best. As the business landscape continues to evolve, EI will remain a key differentiator for organizational resilience and adaptability.

Global and Cultural Implications

The future of emotional intelligence also involves understanding its global and cultural implications. As we become more interconnected, the ability to navigate cultural differences with empathy and respect is paramount. EI can facilitate cross-cultural communication and collaboration, helping to bridge divides and promote mutual understanding.

Moreover, as societies grapple with complex global challenges, such as climate change and social inequality, emotional intelligence can play a role in fostering collective action and resilience. By cultivating empathy and compassion, individuals and communities can work together to address pressing issues and create a more sustainable and equitable world.

The Ongoing Journey of Emotional Intelligence

As we envision the future of emotional intelligence, it is important to recognize that EI is a dynamic and evolving field. Continued research and innovation will deepen our understanding of EI and its applications across various domains. As new insights emerge, individuals and organizations will have the opportunity to refine their approaches to emotional intelligence, enhancing its impact and effectiveness.

In conclusion, the future of emotional intelligence is bright and full of potential. By embracing EI, we can navigate the complexities of the modern world with greater understanding, empathy, and resilience. As we continue to develop and apply emotional intelligence, we have the opportunity to create a more compassionate, connected, and thriving global community.

Final Reflections

As we conclude this exploration into the depths of

emotional intelligence, it's important to recognize that the journey toward developing EI is both personal and universal. Emotional intelligence is not just a skill set to be acquired; it is a lifelong pursuit that enriches every aspect of our lives. It is a journey marked by continuous learning, self-discovery, and transformation.

Embracing the Journey

Developing emotional intelligence begins with a commitment to self-awareness and an openness to change. It requires us to look inward, to confront our vulnerabilities, and to embrace our strengths. This process can be challenging, as it often involves unlearning long-held patterns and beliefs that no longer serve us. Yet, it is through this introspection that we gain clarity and insight into who we are and who we aspire to be.

As you embark on this journey, remember that growth is not linear. There will be moments of progress and setbacks, triumphs and challenges. Each experience is an opportunity to learn and evolve. By approaching each moment with curiosity and compassion, we can navigate the complexities of our emotions and relationships with grace and resilience.

The Ripple Effect of Emotional Intelligence

The impact of emotional intelligence extends beyond the individual. As we cultivate EI within ourselves, we influence those around us, creating a ripple effect that can transform our communities and organizations.

Emotionally intelligent individuals inspire others to connect more deeply, communicate more effectively, and collaborate more harmoniously. They foster environments where empathy and understanding are valued, leading to stronger, more cohesive teams and communities.

In the workplace, emotionally intelligent leaders drive innovation and engagement by creating cultures of trust and inclusivity. They recognize the unique strengths of each team member and empower them to contribute their best. As organizations increasingly prioritize emotional intelligence, they unlock the potential for greater creativity, productivity, and success.

Emotional Intelligence in a Changing World

In a world that is constantly evolving, emotional intelligence is more important than ever. As we face global challenges and navigate technological advancements, the ability to understand and manage emotions is crucial for building a more compassionate and connected world. Emotional intelligence equips us to bridge cultural divides, resolve conflicts, and collaborate across differences.

Moreover, as artificial intelligence and automation reshape industries, the uniquely human qualities of empathy, creativity, and emotional insight will become even more valuable. Emotional intelligence will be a key differentiator, enabling individuals and organizations to thrive in an increasingly complex landscape.

A Call to Action

As you reflect on the insights and strategies shared in this book, I encourage you to take action. Begin by integrating emotional intelligence practices into your daily life. Set aside time for self-reflection, engage in active listening, and practice empathy in your interactions. Seek out opportunities for learning and growth, and be open to feedback and new perspectives.

Remember that emotional intelligence is a journey, not a destination. It is a lifelong commitment to becoming the best version of yourself and contributing positively to the world around you. By cultivating EI, you are not only enhancing your own life but also creating a ripple effect that can lead to a more empathetic, understanding, and connected world.

May this book serve as a guide and inspiration as you continue your journey of developing emotional intelligence. Embrace the opportunities for learning and transformation, and let EI be a guiding force in your pursuit of a fulfilling and successful life.

References

As we conclude our journey through the multifaceted world of emotional intelligence (EI), it is essential to acknowledge the foundational works and contemporary research that have informed our understanding. This chapter provides a list of references and further reading materials for those interested in delving deeper into the study and application of emotional intelligence.

Foundational Works on Emotional Intelligence

1. **Goleman, Daniel.** *Emotional Intelligence: Why It Can Matter More Than IQ.* New York: Bantam Books, 1995.
   - This seminal work by Daniel Goleman brought emotional intelligence into the

mainstream, highlighting its importance in personal and professional success.

2. **Salovey, Peter, and John D. Mayer.** "Emotional Intelligence." *Imagination, Cognition, and Personality* 9, no. 3 (1990): 185-211.
   - The original paper by Salovey and Mayer that introduced the concept of emotional intelligence, defining it as a form of social intelligence.

3. **Goleman, Daniel, Richard Boyatzis, and Annie McKee.** *Primal Leadership: Realizing the Power of Emotional Intelligence.* Boston: Harvard Business Review Press, 2002.
   - This book explores how leaders can harness emotional intelligence to create resonant organizations and drive positive change.

Contemporary Research and Applications

4. **Bar-On, Reuven.** *The Bar-On Emotional Quotient Inventory (EQ-i): A Test of Emotional Intelligence.* Toronto: Multi-Health Systems, 1997.
   - An assessment tool developed to measure emotional intelligence across various dimensions, widely used in research and practice.

5. **Caruso, David R., and Peter Salovey.** *The Emotionally Intelligent Manager: How to Develop and Use the Four Key Emotional Skills of Leadership.* San Francisco: Jossey-Bass, 2004.
   - A practical guide for managers to develop

emotional intelligence skills and apply them effectively in leadership roles.

6. **Bradberry, Travis, and Jean Greaves.** *Emotional Intelligence 2.0.* San Diego: TalentSmart, 2009.
   - This book offers a step-by-step program for increasing emotional intelligence using a variety of strategies and assessments.

Emotional Intelligence in Education

7. **Durlak, Joseph A., Roger P. Weissberg, Allison B. Dymnicki, Rebecca D. Taylor, and Kriston B. Schellinger.** "The Impact of Enhancing Students' Social and Emotional Learning: A Meta-Analysis of School-Based Universal Interventions." *Child Development* 82, no. 1 (2011): 405-432.
   - A comprehensive meta-analysis examining the effects of social-emotional learning programs on students' outcomes.

8. **Elias, Maurice J., et al.** *Promoting Social and Emotional Learning: Guidelines for Educators.* Alexandria: Association for Supervision and Curriculum Development, 1997.
   - Guidelines for integrating social and emotional learning into educational curricula to enhance students' emotional intelligence.

Emotional Intelligence in the Workplace

9. **Cherniss, Cary, and Daniel Goleman, eds.** *The*

Emotionally Intelligent Workplace: How to Select for, Measure, and Improve Emotional Intelligence in Individuals, Groups, and Organizations. San Francisco: Jossey-Bass, 2001.

- A collection of essays exploring the role of emotional intelligence in workplace success and strategies for enhancing EI in organizational settings.

10. **Ashkanasy, Neal M., Charmine E.J. Härtel, and Wilfred J. Zerbe, eds.** *Emotions in Organizational Behavior.* Mahwah: Lawrence Erlbaum Associates, 2005.

- An in-depth exploration of the role of emotions in organizational behavior and the impact of emotional intelligence on workplace dynamics.

Further Reading and Exploration

11. **Siegel, Daniel J.** *The Developing Mind: How Relationships and the Brain Interact to Shape Who We Are.* New York: Guilford Press, 1999.

- A look at how interpersonal relationships and emotional intelligence influence brain development and personal growth.

12. **Kabat-Zinn, Jon.** *Wherever You Go, There You Are: Mindfulness Meditation in Everyday Life.* New York: Hyperion, 1994.

- A guide to mindfulness meditation and its role in enhancing self-awareness and emotional regulation.

13. **Brown, Brené.** *Daring Greatly: How the Courage to Be Vulnerable Transforms the Way We Live, Love,*

Parent, and Lead. New York: Gotham Books, 2012.

- An exploration of vulnerability and its connection to emotional intelligence, offering insights into building authentic and resilient relationships.

Conclusion

This collection of references and further reading materials provides a comprehensive foundation for understanding and applying emotional intelligence. As you continue your journey of developing EI, these resources can offer valuable insights and guidance. Whether you are a leader, educator, coach, or individual seeking personal growth, the study of emotional intelligence is a rewarding and enriching endeavour.

M A. Grant

ABOUT THE AUTHOR

M A. Grant is a dedicated and motivated values driven individual, he has mentored leaders and supported organizations as they shape and develop their leadership styles and cultural identities.

He has more than twenty years strategic, advisory and operational experience in the fields of leadership, management and corporate innovation. This has stretched across a wide range of international governmental and private sector organizations.

He has a genuine interest in personnel development and the growth of human capital with a proven ability to unleash people's real potential.

.